Silent Clouds: A Poetry Collection

By Olivia Camara

Table of CONTENTS

Preface

This collection is a snapshot of a specific time in my life. It was written throughout my childhood and teenage years without the goal of crafting a book. I had no intention of having an audience at the time. Instead, these pieces were attempts to process the wonder, confusion, and fears I faced while growing up. As a whole, they capture the feelings of navigating the new experiences of adulthood and the loss of childhood. To me, it's a time capsule of my emotions during a time that seems excessively emotional.

I know that as I grow older, my perspective will shift, and I'll probably look back at these with a lot more nostalgia and maybe some embarrassment, but I find that level of honesty beautiful. My goal in sharing it is to show a reflection of fairly average, yet raw, messy, human emotions and I hope that as a reader you can find a piece of yourself in these poems, or at least remember the feeling of being young.

Thank you for sharing these memories with me.

Love

*"...what you say, has arisen out of a confusion of **love** and the **beloved**, which made you think that love was all beautiful."*
-Plato, Symposium

How Dare I Breathe

A golden ray drops like honey from the sky above me.
It *bleeds* through *leaves*
A green glowing canopy.
My back rests on the hard shingles of the roof
Teardrops slipping towards my ear.
The mass of sunlight creeps down the sky
Melts into the horizon as always.
Does it know that when it rose this morning your lungs took a breath?
Does it know that as it slips away tonight your tired lungs are still?
Empty
The air grows cold
And the honey droplets of sunlight on leaves evaporate.
Sparkles pierce the black sky now
And the cold air fills *my* lungs.
How dare I breathe.
How dare I feel the night air on my skin
How dare I shiver while your body feels nothing.
I yearn for the day not to end
For the world to cease its spinning
How dare it go on.
Moonlight pours down from above
Like a river from my eyes.
A sort of hollowness weighs on my chest.
Have you felt it
Or do you feel it now?
My lungs threaten to collapse
As the air is too sweet.
Do I dare breathe?

The Love Cycle

I've often heard it said

That love is wonderfully dangerous.
An illness,
That slips through nostrils disguised as cheap cologne
Through hopeful eyes and giggling mouths.
A brush of an elbow,
An inside joke.
A dreamy haze,
In which you cannot distinguish dedication from desire.

It is fearing loss.
Fearing silence on the end of a phone line
Pouring syllables to fill a quiet gap,
And gifting every corner of yourself.

It is picking up shards of the self respect
Your father spent your childhood crafting,
Because you mistook love for lust.

It is attachment intertwined with addiction,
Constant withdrawal and relapse.

It is placing your soft heart in prickly hands,
Yet wondering how it has been punctured.

It is spilling sour feelings you do not understand
Nor dare to express from your tongue,
Through ink on clean parchment,

But then again, seeing the universe in their eyes.

Strangers

I once believed that one can't *know* a stranger
Once approached they become a friend,
A lover, or enemy.
I've been taught that's simply a trend.
How can I know someone's mind like it's my own,
Read them like a note worlds away,
Help them at their best and worst
Never sugar coat saying, "please stay".
Begging "please stay", whether night or day
When we know that's not right, but we say it's ok.
How can I care for one person with all of my being?
Hoping his heart was poured out
Over messages I'm re-reading.
And even though he spit his hate
And even though he's feasted on sorrow
Caused wounds I can't articulate
And emotions that scrape my throat as I swallow
I can't forget about when he cared.
When he gazed upon my face
And didn't look, but stared.
When there was nothing he would not give for me
When it seemed as if he could have *died* for me
But somehow couldn't live beside me.
Disney taught us
What is broken can be fixed by a *kiss*
But there was something I must've *missed.*
Because after all the love I poured out and shared
After efforts to avoid all dangers
We have a million memories
But we're *still* strangers

So yes
I can know someone
More than they know themselves
But after love and tears
I must put memories back on shelves
I must pretend I can't notice one face in a riot
Pretend I don't recognize one voice
Worlds away when it's quiet.
And we'll live in silence,
Two strangers sharing a lifetime of memories.

Waiting

A stuffy aroma,
Latex gloves,
And rubbing alcohol,
Heavy in my lungs.

A sickening gleam,
Fluorescent lights reflecting
Off cinder block walls
Causing my head to throb.

Screams of squeaky shoes
Echo down endless halls.
The hospital swallows me whole.

Nauseous from the drive
I sit
Legs dangling from an itchy waiting room chair

Minutes bleed by.
I imagine he's bleeding on hospital sheets.

I blink.

Shove the image of his limp body
In the pouring rain from my mind.

The clock on the wall ticks.
It ticks
It ticks

My ears can't help but notice it's ticking,
Identical to the pattering raindrops
On his broken helmet.

People come and go.
Paying no attention to the child waiting alone
Nor the droplet tracing a sticky path down her face.

One tear.

One tear,
Yet the whole ocean seems to sit in my throat.
I swallow hard, anxious to the point of exhaustion.

Eyes glued
To the dimly lit fish tank
Feeling trapped
One goldfish
Swims circles in her glass prison.

Limerence

He had a mansion within my mind.
Where he lived with wealth
Day and night, whether I rose or slept.
Unwelcomed at the door,
Yet somehow he took up every nook and void of my being.
I sensed his presence in a crowded room
From glimpses of familiar fabric
And the gentle waft of musty cologne.

My spine crawled.

He had a mansion within my mind
That I had not built nor asked him to reside.
But the touch of skin and the infatuation of a smile is not always invited.
I could ponder words or paint worlds within my head
But rather his presence sat like vicious fumes
Rotting my skull as I lied it on silk pillows
Waiting for shared sentiment
A message I would never receive.

If limerence could heal, he would live forever
Yet he did not notice me in a crowded room,
Not me nor the familiar fabric I ironed,
And the sweet perfume I hoped he'd remember.
The mansion within my mind grew vacant
Saved for the hologram of the person I wished he was.

Starry Night

Deep eyes hold a night sky full of stars.
His gaze could leave me enchanted or bleak,
Yet I trade my loneliness for scars
those stars–plummet, like teardrops on my cheek.

His tainted words prick my tender heart
As I lay in the lush field of thoughts
Wondering if he paints lies like art
With my trustless mind, my stomach in knots.

Empty promises like shooting stars fly
Gleaming yet meaningless, becoming my bane
Leaving me under that desolate sky
Cold, yet comforted by the drizzling rain.

But still I love on, ignoring his lies.
Trapped in the Starry Night held in his eyes.

In the late 1700's, William Wordsworth published a group of poems titled, "Lucy" describing a beautiful girl that he fell in love with who mysteriously died. In reality, Lucy never existed. She was a symbol of the memories he had, from all of the women he had admired, loved, and lost throughout his life. Psychologists hypothesize that memories attached to one's "first love" might create paths in an individual's brain that are strikingly similar to that of memories causing PTSD. They are believed to be often permanent, and are memories one subconsciously refers back to forever, regardless of how much love and joy an individual shares with others. This study and Wordsworth poetry inspired "The Memories".

The Memories

His life was quiet, stable, repetitive.
Just as common as the sun peaking over the horizon,
was his wife, pouring steaming coffee into a white mug, and placing buttered
toast on the table.

His home was sturdy, warm.
On Sundays he yelled at the football game on TV, on Tuesdays he watched
western reruns, his wife knitting quietly beside him until the room inevitably
grew too loud for her.

He felt guilt.
Seeing her silently wince as his voice competed with the commentator across
the room. She would lay her knitting on the couch and make dinner.
Their kids had grown up between these walls, and although they lived across
the country now, his memories of their giggling still echoed through the halls.

He loved them dearly, and he *was* happy,
But despite being thoroughly satisfied with his life,
with his family, with his home, the dull days, the quiet;

He couldn't help but think of Lucy.
Her face appeared to him in dreams and memories,
her wind blown blond hair, with hints of brunette hidden between the strands,
Her huge brown eyes searched for his and creased when she laughed too
loud.
It was decades ago now, before bills and back pain,
And yet when he drove too fast he still thought of Lucy,
standing on the passenger seat, her head out of the sun roof.
Laughing as she struggled to take a breath,
her lungs filled with wind and hair whipping her face.

When the music seemed too loud, he thought of Lucy
Her french tipped fingers cranking the volume,
Screaming along to words he wished he knew.

It was decades ago and yet,
He still sensed the excitement of being beside Lucy,
As she'd twirl and dance in the middle of the streets, a band would play on
the corner and cars would honk, waiting for her to move.
She didn't care.

He remembered when he reached for his umbrella
Lucy grabbed his hand and dragged him into the downpour.
She leaped into a puddle
Her sun dress soaked her smile beaming.
The thought of jumping into the rain to him was senseless
But the stream running down his back, filling his shoes, soaking his socks
was freedom if Lucy was there with him.

He remembered his mother calling her wild
He remembered his heart, pounding every time her gentle eyes met his
He remembered the adrenaline
Shooting through his body as he followed her into anything.
He remembered his love
His *first* love.

And couldn't help but wonder what lives he would have lived,
If he hadn't left the excitement, the rush, and warm pleasure of her presence,
If the jewel that *was* Lucy had not slipped between his fingers.

Flowers

A presence like a butterfly
Unheard, gently passive.
He drew no attention when he entered a room.

Grand thoughts and little words,
Sunken eyes that searched for answers
In shifting, sneering faces.
Mother told him to treat others how he wanted to be treated.
And so he kept salutations to himself
And hid behind a plethora of knowledge.
He found that functions, formulas, and facts did not frighten him
The way that handshakes and hellos could.

He *was* a butterfly.
Hidden among the flowers
A warmth to those who searched for delicate
wings
And mosaics of color.
The world did not notice
Nor miss his gentle presence
When they laid him under the flowers.
Yet I did.

My heart ceased its fluttering,
And the world grew slightly colder.
While staring out my frosted window,
I wondered
If he grew colder with it,
As his body lay under the flowers.

Growing Pains

Days spent spreading schoolyard whispers
And sharing playground giggles
Were spent with him.
When nothing mattered,
But the sun on our backs
And the ball in our hands.
Inside jokes that stemmed from childish humor
And grew like vines intertwining our minds.
Our legs carrying us through mossy meadows
My speed matched his
We didn't know that wouldn't last forever
There was nothing we believed we could not do.
We would grow up together
And hold our dreams in cupped hands
Like glasswork that shimmered when we held it to starlight.

Our dreams stayed in cupped hands.
While our bodies were drawn apart,
I naively thought our minds would somehow stay connected from childhood.
And learned that holding fragile dreams
Meant turning a back to the children we were
Departing from the warmth of his side.

Our eyes would no longer meet
His dream would be placed into another's hands
And she'd learn to laugh and cry beside him just as I did.
Although she did not know him yet
And would never know him the way that I did
Nor have the childish memories of schoolyard giggles
Passing classroom notes, hopscotch, and holding hands,

As I stepped away from him for the last time,
I hoped that she would cherish growing old with him
As much as I cherished growing up with him.

His Book

The crack of the spine as I opened the book.
A scent like soil, bleach, and wet ink.
His name in bold letters
Under a swirly script cursive title.
I did not breathe.

But instead soaked up every printed word.
Though there was a galaxy between us
And he would not dare to breathe *my* name
Nor risk an eye in *my* direction.
I still held this book.
His name on the cover,
And a glimpse into the world of his mind between the pages.
Prepared to endure poetry like blades to the gut,
I turned a page to read.

"I think of her and only remember warmth of rest like cotton hoodies and hot chocolate, Safety of laughter like a head on a shoulder or a thumb brushing tears from puffy red eyes. Where she saw hurt I saw love that slipped like sand through our hourglass."

That's all he wrote.
I let damp pages slide from my fingers,
And closed the spine again.

ROSES

Red petals pure blood,
On sharp thorny stems,
Sit vibrant and lively in
Every man's hand as they
Stand at the door, claiming they love.

The Art of Casual Affection

Casual affection was not in my vocabulary.

I was not taught to love a little.
Subtle hands intertwined and empty hugs
Meaningless conversations that exposed the depths of our souls
My forehead on your neck and the comfort of silence.

                    ***

I was not taught to love small,
So when you held me and wiped the sorrow from my cheek
I searched for a future in your eyes,
And took the burden from your back.

I gently held the secrets you shared
And relished the trust you gifted me
Like painted porcelain
That could fall to pieces at my smallest mistake.

As my mother taught me,
I assumed the best of you
And forgave and forgot every error.
I was not taught to love a little.

So when you held my head to your beating heart
But walked past me like a stranger unseen,

When you whispered that you could not live without my smile
But continued on, when you saw woe upon my lips
I did not understand.

That's not how I saw my father treat my mother.
That's not how I thought affection was shown.

I could not love small.
So if I could not love you with every crevice of my being
Lend my hand when the world scrapes at your chest
Search for the comfort of your face in a crowd
And keep you like you were the lifeline for my drowning lungs,
Then I could not love you at all.

Truth

"The truth is rarely pure and never simple…"
- Oscar Wilde, *The Importance of Being Earnest*

Mother of Pearl

From youthful eyes she was no different than an artifact.
Wisps of white hair sat like helpless clouds upon her pale skull.
Splashes of melanin stained her arms and face.
Her skin, as thin and white as paper, wrinkled as she moved.
An unintentional and regretful disgust
Seeped into a child's mind as she spoke.
Her voice, a breathy *croak*
Escaping from her esophagus,
Was an undemanding mutter,
A disregarded string of words,
Lost in the slightest ruckus.
From such youthful eyes she was
Ancient, significant, yet irrelevant, and ignored.
In the echo of need however,
When one's soul longed for guidance
With no clear road signs in sight,
Her words were recognized as pearls,
Gleaming as they rolled from between her lips.
Holding a lifetime of wisdom like the layers
Of glittering nacre.
That croaking voice held colorful stories,
Crumbs of sweet knowledge like spiritual nutrition,
Her weary tone was rich in prudence
Only accessible to those who sought diligence.
She was a worn book, faded at the cloth edges,
Torn at the spine, overflowing pages
A wealth of understanding.
Seeming to have all that is to be known,
Yet soon,
Too soon she would be relieved.

She would slip into what is *un*known,
And those who read the lines of her worn pages,
Tasted the sweetness of her presence,
Would carry her memories, her wisdom as if it was their own.
While those swayed away by disgust, would long for such insight.
Such precious pearls.

His Changing Gaze

My father was the first man I knew.
His shoulder was firm, a place to rest my head.
I closed my eyes pretending to sleep
He carried me from the car-seat to bed.
I never talked too much.
I could sit on his lap and he would listen intently.
He was the first man to tell me I was beautiful.
I was too young to understand those words,
Yet he placed them on my head like a glass crown gently;
With no hopes of receiving anything in return.
When I wept he caught my tears,
With his hand rough and worn
From the toil that put food in my stomach.
He rubbed my back and told stories
That put my small mind at ease.
I slipped into slumber
With him crouched at the edge of my bed on tired knees.
He watched over me.
He was comfort.

My big brothers were the next men I knew.
They played tricks on me
And laughed, making my trust quiver.
After school soccer matches
And backyard football games
They knocked me down.
I learned that my strength would never match a man's
But when I fell they picked me back up,
Brushing off my scrapes and cleaning my wounds.
Their arms would always be my safety

And their laughter would be my home.
Although I was young I learned to care for them.
My words could make them smile
My small embrace could cure the sadness behind their brows.

The next man I knew followed the trend.
When I fell he lifted me up,
And brushed me off the way my brothers had.
He caught my tears and told me I was beautiful
Just like my father, though his tone was not the same.
His compliments were drizzled on me
Like honey garnishing a meal
He was hoping to enjoy in return.
I did not understand.
Like my brothers', I saw his arms as my safety
And because of my father, I trusted his worn hands.
They lingered longer than I was used to.
But I translated touch as care.
I thought he must love me more than my father
Because he held me more than my father had
And would carry my sleeping body to bed,
The way my father did, so many years ago.

I soon learned there was a difference in the intention
Though the actions were the same…

He did not watch me with the same eyes my father had.
At some point he stopped catching my tears
And a small embrace was not enough
To cure the thirst behind his brow.
At some point he changed my perception of men.

No longer comfort in a firm shoulder
No longer safety found in rough hands
Danger in the word beautiful
Compliments were now bait
And loving a man became naive.

In 1923, Wallace Stevens published "Thirteen Ways of Looking at a Black Bird" in the poetry collection, "Harmonium". Through this piece Stevens took a seemingly simple topic, a black bird, and described it in thirteen disconnected stanzas numbered with Roman Numerals. By doing this, he captured the creature through 13 drastically different lenses, creating a mosaic effect that illustrated the complexities of both a bird and societal perception. Seventy-two years later, Henry Louis Gates Jr. wrote "Thirteen Ways of Looking at a Black Man", an essay collection that depicted various ways that Black Men are perceived in modern America. Since then, artists have created an array of pieces based off of this concept. They have illustrated objects, people, or concepts that seem simple with thirteen different viewpoints, from Thirteen ways of looking at art to Thirteen ways of looking at a pencil. Their work along with my identity as a biracial America inspired "Thirteen Ways of Looking at Myself'.

Thirteen Ways of Looking at Myself

I
"Exotic"
A stranger's oily fingers
Stroking my petting zoo of curls.

II
"Misplaced"
The confusion in their shifting eyes
Wondering why I share no features
With the colorless hand intertwined with mine.

III
"Black"
Home grown from backyard barbeques
And sunday church choirs where
My melanin made up for my music taste.

IV
"White"
Two lips that mirror an African lineage
Though my way of speaking
Carries my mother's pale shadow.

V
"A statistic"
Teachers hovering over my desk,
Take pride as I check two boxes at once.

VI
"Deceptive"
Born with two mouths
Switch tongues as I enter the room
Constantly molding my personality.

VII
"Unseen"
Lost in the abyss
Between two worlds,
Crushed by two standards.

VIII
"Voiceless"
Each breath from my lungs
Carrying the weight of two stories.

IX
"Traitor"
A heart somehow rooted in pain
Told my heritage
Taught to hate,

X
"Ambivalent",
Tongue twisted until silent
As choosing one side
Would be showing hatred
To a part of myself

XI
"An anomaly",
Faced with the same question at every greeting
Never asked my ethnicity or race
Because my skin color
Drains the life from my veins.
Objectified by a three word sentence
Asked out of ignorance.
"What are you?"

XII
"Free"
A bridge between two oceans
That never seem to blend.

XIII
"Unique"
Understanding all areas of a spectrum
That does not have a spot for me.

TEARS

Two eyes mirroring the milky way,
Empty and infinite, stained glass windows to an
Aching soul.
Rolling down soft rosy cheeks, one crystalline drop falls,
Splashes, and melts into the soil growing flowers.

Fame

Friendly smiles spread across her face,
Captured by a camera
With no explanation for her joy.
Perfect
A title placed with coveting eyes,
A burden thrown across her backs.
Do they not know that mystery hides behind a mother's jewelry,
And deceit is smuggled between a father's words?
Are they aware that a daughter isn't born with a love for reading,
But slips from the blade of reality
Getting lost in the pages of a worn book?
Do they notice how a son's eloquence is self taught
To survive unpredictable waves of a social sea
An iron muzzle shoved over his lips.
The burden of attention upon his shoulder

In the sought after gaze of the public eye
They once sat but now they lie
A veil, a smile
Writing words of what they think but can not say.

Sacrifice

Her smooth black flats, decorated with elegant bows
Clicked with every step down the hall.
I followed behind her, glancing
At worn "hand-me-down" sneakers that clung to my feet.
Though dressed in the same school uniform,
My red polo and khakis,
Spotted and stained, seemed gruesome
Compared to her freshly pressed garments.
Holding open the bathroom door for me,
Her eyes quickly scanned my clothing.
She swiftly looked away,
The way pedestrians look away from beggars,
Hoping I wouldn't speak to her,
Hoping I didn't recognize the pity in her eyes.
I blushed.
Rushing towards a bathroom stall to find safety,
To my surprise, I found my mother,
On her knees, wisps of hair in her eyes,
Bright yellow gloves on her hands,
Scrubbing the porcelain toilet with all her strength.
She looked up at me
She smiled,
Asking me how my day was and
Suddenly a brand new khaki skirt meant nothing.

Romanticized Infatuation

Although my reflection stares back at me daily in the mirror,
It somehow looks strange now, staring back in the blade.
It's no longer my hand that grips the cool metal handle.
That can't be my breath that I see in the crisp frozen air.
Cold anger surges through my veins, each heartbeat blaring in my ears.
I have no control over the numb legs that carry me.
I close my eyes, letting darkness embrace me.
Nothing.
My eyes now glazed with salty tear drops, blur the world around me
And for just a moment there is peace.
The white dress slowly fades to crimson before me.
My shaking hands slide the weapon from the fabric and I stare at it again
My reflection has returned, now dripping red.
My hands are finally mine, stained and dirty.

More

Clean clothes cling to his back
An unwavering roof faces storms above him.
His stomach has never moaned
Nor experienced the pains of vacancy.
When his eyelids begin to droop
A soft pillow catches his head.
And a fur blanket waits to embrace him.
Worlds of knowledge lay at his fingertips
Eager to be explored.
Behind the eyes of many, he must be a king.

There is nothing he lacks, yet from his own eyes,
He sees a void.
He longs for an infinite amount of crinkled cloth to fill it.
Like paper to the touch, yet like glory to the mind.
Stained green yet faded by the hands it has passed
through.
Holding the faint aroma of ink and power.

He searches cool coins,
That metallic scent of copper,
The familiar clinking as they fall into deep pockets,
And the subtle weight of value.

A desire, that strengthens his limbs
So he may hike mountains and fight battles to
achieve more
Help others, not out of compassion but out of a need
for more
He spins traps like the webs of an arachnid

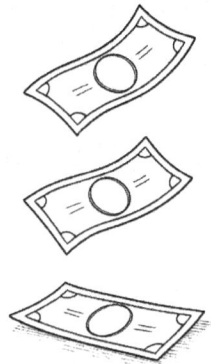

So that he may snatch the few treasures held by the others
And feed his insatiable thirst for more.

His vision blurs to green,
As he wastes away, counting zeros.
Mere comfort is no longer comfortable enough
And thriving is no longer adequate.
Loving hands are now obstacles
On the journey towards wealth.

He will find himself,
In all his glory,
Drowning in the green luscious foliage of riches,
Surrounded by no one.

No Place Like

When I was 5
I knew every corner, crevice, and crack of my home.
Like cloud watching I stared at the smudges in the ceiling paint
Until I could make out shapes and faces.
There was endless magic between the walls.
A polyester blanket was a fortress roof top
A plastic serving spoon became a hockey stick.
There was nothing else to the world beyond my street.

When I was 6
I stared out of foggy window panels,
Watched clouds drag across a bland sky
Until there was no sky left to creep across
They disappeared beyond what I could see.
And I wondered where that was.
The scratches in the wood of my bedroom door never changed.
The wind could make my whole world creak.
I lived in a glass bottle of a home,
I watched the street lights flicker
And strangers walk lazily past my yard
But from where?

When I was 8
The porch door was where I spent my hours
Filling my nostrils with clean spring air.
Cars zoomed past my sleepy street,
All different colors and shapes
With different people inside.
I wondered where they were going,

Did they feel the same restlessness that crawled up through my knees
I wanted to chase behind them, like a puppy chasing butterflies,
I knew there was no use, but I felt
That there was something I was missing out on.

When I was 9
That restlessness trembled through my fingers like a scared spider
As I unlocked the handle
And slipped out of those porch doors.
I sprinted away, determined to leave.
I turned right, and right again, and again.
Somehow I ended up back at my home
"Was the bottle shrinking or was I growing?"
I asked through panting breaths.

When I was 10
I went to sleepovers
A whole new world, their windows were bigger
They had trinkets that I couldn't afford.
Soon the secret faces in the ceiling smudges
Had disappeared, I only saw dirt my mother could not reach.

When I was 15
I climbed onto a plane.
that carried me over sparkly cities and neatly placed suburbs.
I was among the clouds
What I had dreamed of was at my fingertips.
I landed in a city of voices, music, and color.
Bodies, smoke, and chaos.
Spring air now had aromas that made my mouth water and nose wrinkle.
A man on the corner threw paint on to a canvas
And yet the streets walked on

His art at our feet.
A woman poured unfathomable melody from her tongue,
Like liquid gold to my ears
Beauty rang through her speakers
Yet the world had no time to listen
Too many places to go
Too many things to look at.

Grand chaos, colossal noise,
It drowned the voice from my lungs
If I screamed I would not be heard,
I was miniscule compared to the world I had been dropped into.

Now as an adult
I claw past crowds of people
To climb into a plane,
Past the heavenly music
The sweet aromas
And the divine cotton clouds.
So that I may find my way
Back home
Where the crickets chirp can be heard in the night
And spring still taints the air with sweet nectar.
The sky still rains with stars
And the clouds still roll by lazily.

And yet it seems too late.
The shelter, the comfort,
Is no longer for me.

Beauty

"Beauty is the mark God sets upon virtue."
        -Ralph Waldo Emerson, *Nature*

Famous Insecurities

Gazing into a portrait framed by lightbulbs
Fame stares back at her.
Artists swarming her like mosquitos,
Her face the canvas.
They brush thick paint,
Hiding her imperfections with a mask
Of concealer and lipstick.
Hands grabbing, tugging at her hair,
Supposedly fixing it
As if it were once broken.
Spraying sweet smelling chemicals
They suffocate her lungs.
Each insult, a dagger
Between her shoulder blades
Eating away at her waist.
She's now a flawless hourglass,
A rotting apple core.
A sea of clicking cameras swallows her,
Flashing lights turn her way.
Arms reaching for her,
Voices screaming her name.
With a plastered smile
She waves a gentle hand,
Searching for faces in the crowd.
Though seeing only a strange reflection
In gleaming lenses,
A reflection that is no longer her own.
Hollywood rips the heart from her chest
A lifeless body printed on magazine covers
Where every little girl longs to be.

Safety of Fabric

"Too short, too low, too tight",
The phrases that slip from my mother's lips like ropes
Twisting around my wrists,
Confining me to thick baggy fabrics
Yet I see recognition in her eyes
And relief as she zips a hoodie around my body
Like a bullet proof vest.

"It's not a fashion show"
A sour remark that falls heavy from my father's throat
As I spin in front of my reflection
Fear sits in his eyes as he embraces me,
A temporary shelter.

I laugh at their worry,
And assure them that I'm confident enough
To disregard others' opinions.

Confidence fuels my strut
Aware and proud of the eyes I draw.
Yet soon the positive loving attention
Morphs into a twisted absorption.

Rather than eyes of appreciation,
Eyes of hunger fall upon me,
Starving lips call my name,
My body like a fruitless meal meant to be enjoyed
By those who see and crave it.

Suddenly I long to be wrapped in that heavy fabric by my mother
And escape to the warmth and shelter of my father's embrace.

Snow

A colorless sky above one's head.
A faded ground below
A dull array of broken twigs
A barren stretch of dead grass

It is a graveyard of fallen leaves
Dried up and discolored
That crunch beneath a footstep
And roll like tumbleweeds in the screaming
wind.

Bare trees sway and creak
As if crying out into the ghost land
Their empty branches are the fingers of a
skeleton
Bursting from the frozen earth.

Thick clouds cast a murky darkness
Veiling the sun's face
From the dreary fields
No light, No warmth, No foliage, No
flowers.

But as if it were a miracle,
A fluffy speck descends from the hollow
heavens.
Glistening crystals begin to rain upon the dead world like falling stars.
Landing again and again forming mounds of pure cotton
Piling up on trees, bushes, twigs, and rooftops.
Soon the world is covered by a glittering white blanket

Reflecting the little light left by the hidden sun.
The white sheet hugs earth like a made bed
Untouched, untainted.

It is the same colorless sky above
And the same broken twigs below.
Under the silent frozen bed.
The grass is still a crunchy bed of brown.

Yet the world has somehow awoken.

Blinded By Books

Lead between your fingers,
The monotonous scratching of marks on a line.
Though breathtaking meadows and rolling hills are visible
Just out the window to your right
Your head hangs down.
Your eyes do not dare to slide away
From the words between your two hands.
The squeaking of vibrant polymer
Slipping across a floor-to-ceiling whiteboard,
And the alcoholic scent that bleeds
From an Expo's felt tip.
It is all *too* familiar.

Flickering lights, white walls, and wooden desks,
An underpaid man in an oversized suit feeding you words
You must swallow and regurgitate on a paper next week.
This is success.
Your mind, like a universe holding worlds you have somehow formed
Your mind, shaped and reshaped by experiences,
Is measured on a scale, A to F by a ball-point pen on parchment.
That is success.
Mentally race the peers you sit 12 inches from.
Assess their weaknesses and strengths
As they assess yours, subconsciously pray that you excel and hope that they
struggle.
This is success?
And after sleepless nights toiling under lamp light wrenching your weary
eyelids open,
Despite the bed being just beside you; relief seeps into your stomach,
replacing sharp fear

Once you receive a score that validates your mind, telling you that you are *not* stupid.
That is joy.
Not a sweet joy, but the bitter joy of victory while others fall behind you,
Painful joy of knowing your struggles were worth something.
Worth a score.
From A to F.
That's the track that you are placed on.
Without your consent you are thrown into a game that you must to learn to win
In order to experience and re-experience that joy,

*   *   *

Yet there's another joy.
Though daring to appreciate its fresh freedoms, pulls you to the rear of the race you must win.
The simple joy found in beauty.

A joy you feel when gazing to the sky.
As it mirrors the ocean's infinite azure, a unique artwork that forms each evening as paint Brushes splash colors across the canvas sky.
The sun, plunging into still waters, leaving a trail of blues, purples, and pinks behind.
The magic of stars, that hang like frozen fireworks,
Far away night lights sparkle as if laughing at you.
The rushing sound of wind shattering the leaves, like a waterfall in the sky.
The secret songs of birds that call to one another as they glide overhead.
The dance of butterflies, that float aimlessly, and the color glimmering off their backs.

Contagious joy

A baby's laugh,
That spreads from cheek to cheek,
To their squinting eyes, and soon to yours.

The warmth of touch

Your hand slipping into another's, feeling a heartbeat through fingertips
Knowing those fingertips feel yours too.

The beauty in conversation.

Sharing parts of yourself
As you venture into the depths of another's mind through their words.
Dancing with the emotions that fill them,
And offering the safety of your presence.

The joy of life.
Such satisfaction thought to be found in success,
Such satisfaction that is sought after
In poorly lit libraries, dusty books, and quiet classrooms,
Surrounds us like the sweet oxygen that fills our lungs.

Goodbyes

"Hi" was probably the first thing I said to her.
No passion, nor meaning behind the word.
A two letter escape from discomfort
An attempt to make an ally.
Small, meaningless, it launched me head first into a
Shallow conversation.
She lived somewhere on the map
I hadn't been there.
She didn't know where my city was either.
We smiled,
Faked a laugh
At jokes that weren't funny.
Desperately avoiding silence,
Grasping for common interests in the dark
Breaking ice as much as two strangers could
We swapped contacts.
She was then a number in my phone,
A name that I repeated in a mutter when she turned away
I hoped I would remember
Or maybe recognize the freckle on her left cheek.
She wasn't memorable.
She wasn't interesting.
But maybe she would provide a seat at a table.
Home was no longer an option
But maybe a morsel of comfort
Of familiarity would be found in her presence.
I saw her again.
She said "hello"
This time out of hope

That I might have remembered the empty conversation we shared.
It wasn't that, but the freckle on her cheek.
I smiled, said hello
Excited to no longer be alone.
I saw her again and again.

*   *   *

It should have been as simple as saying hi.
A meaningless word
A polite normalized gesture
But telling her goodbye was like tearing a bandaid
Off of a fresh open gash.
It was not just one word.
It was her arms around my neck,
Tears dampening each other's cheeks.
Her face turned red and I didn't just see a freckle on a left cheek
But a story that I had learned and loved.
She was not just a companion to past the time
Nor an open seat at a breakfast table.
She had replaced what I formerly called home.
We shared the same breathe a thousand times
The same memories of sleepless nights and painful mornings.
We were two different bodies
But I could not imagine her heart
Beating on the other side of the earth from mine.
I could not imagine her life going on behind my back
Like a show, I was no longer allowed to watch.
Her voice, a song that I was no longer allowed to hear.
It was not that I would miss her.
But that I would be plunged back into a sea of solitary
I would grope in darkness without the lifeline she had become.

Goodbye was not the last thing I said to her.
We had become like one
And when I looked into her glazed eyes there
Were infinite words that passed between us.
Her footsteps carried her away,
Rolling a suitcase behind.
I watched her go….knowing our eyes would never meet again.